Kitty cat
and the paint

Story by Annette Smith

Illustrations by Ben Spiby

2

Kitty Cat looked out the window.

She saw Fat Cat

asleep in the sun.

She saw some red paint, too.

Kitty Cat went outside.

She went to look at the paint.

"Meow!" said Kitty Cat.

"Look at this!"

Fat Cat woke up.

"Go away, Kitty Cat," he said.
"You woke me up.
Go away, and let me sleep
in the sun."

"Meow!" said Kitty Cat.

"I'm not going away.

I'm going to look in here."

Kitty Cat looked at the paint.

Fat Cat got up.

His back went up!

"Go away, Kitty Cat,"
said Fat Cat.
"You are very naughty."

Fat Cat ran to get Kitty Cat.

Kitty Cat ran fast.

She ran back inside the house,

and she got away

from Fat Cat.

But Fat Cat ran too fast.

Crash!

The red paint

went onto the grass.

Fat Cat ran into the paint
and he got it on his paws.

"Look at the paint on the sidewalk," said Kitty Cat.

"Fat Cat is naughty!"